Under Aurora Skies

D. Tru`stone

BookLeaf
Publishing

India | USA | UK

Made with ❤ on the BookLeaf Publishing Platform
www.bookleafpub.in
www.bookleafpub.com

Dedication

I dedicate this to "KissenKitten",

For nearly breaking my spirit, and motivation to
continue writing so many years ago.
May the stars provide you clearer context than these
words ever will, and the aurora's dances bring upon you
a renewed vibrancy.

Preface

I am Tru`stone a poet and aspiring visual artist *(TheAuroraOro)*.

I've written over two thousand five hundred poems since 2004, with over a thousand posted on my Art's Community discord server, the Oro's Pen. My journey into visual art began late 2021, as an art lover I created a space for artists and authors to share their works, grow, and guide others to pursue, improve, and impress within their own journeys.

Poetry is and has always been an outlet to my emotions and musings, a creative thread to slip along with whenever inspiration struck from the most unlikely of sources, a select few of these within this collection inspired by the dinosaur survival game: **The Isle**.

Do settle with me by the rivers of Lune, and let us both listen to the songs within these fluttering leafs under aurora skies.

Cover Art by TheAuroraOro (D. Tru`stone)

Acknowledgements

The artistic journey starts with a single thought,
a single step, and a single line.
it is a journey, an endeavor, an epic.

There are many inspiring artists and authors out there,
you may not be able to attain their performance,
but with practice, with effort, and determination,
you'll ind your medium through experimentation,
you'll gain the innovation to venture into the unknown,
you'll confidently hone your craft, build your rhythm,

and all those artists and authors you had followed -
you'll become as one alongside them -
and could one day inspire them as much as they had
inspired you.

This work wouldn't be possible without the support of
my friends, supporters, and fellow authors and artists.

1. Tapestry

Take every little thought,
every little breath,
every little little,
every little line -

and draw them upon the open canvas
of the skies,
of pages white;
upon your heart

and bring forth the image,
whether through a thousand words,
or a thousand colors,
into a tapestry fine.

2. Traverse

Travel with me to the lands beyond the Pale,
roam with me through the meadows I hail,
approach with me the shimmering skyline
vibrantly dancing to welcome you and I.

escape with me into the lunar skies,
roam with me to where the aurora lies,
sing with me into the mighty gale
the echoes of the Eld beyond the Pale.

3. Aurora's Song

Into the solar winds,
we set our course -
where the old world ends,
the new world begins,
we follow the tides
through the black and white,
cradled by her wings
we seek the light;

The songs of silence
she sent so long,
to seek the guidance
to hold her strong
determined defiance
against all gone wrong,
for the last of the titans
brings Aurora's song

So find the stars
to bring you day,
to guide you far
through the milkyway,
for your wings to spread
and your voice be heard,
beyond the waves of dread
and seas of hurt -

The songs of silence
she sent so long,
to seek the guidance
to hold her strong
determined defiance
against all gone wrong;
for the last of the titans
brings Aurora's song

4. Touch

To the moment,
a gentle sensation ,
upon the wind,
a breath of elation,
a gentle beat
of anticipation,
a chorus brings
greater inspiration

To the moment,
a touch of innovation,
upon the wind
a greater motivation
offers the beat
to end self damnation
as the chorus brings
its divine salvation.

5. A New Poem

A thought by the candle light,

No emotions tonight,
even while there's so much to write,
why are these words not flowing right?

Perhaps the motions are too tight,
oh! Perhaps it's the loss of sight,
even now the Touch is experiencing the plight,
mayhap the author losing their might?

A dreadful cycle,

not I place I wished to go,
everything pains, aches, and feels slow,
why-ever have it come to this fading glow?

Perhaps my motions are too tight I know,
over these uncertainties and the stressful lows;
with every tide I long to retreat to the meadows:
mayhap find my shelter 'neath these willows.

A dreadful cycle,

to be broken

by a touch of inspiration
by a spark of imagination,
and upon a sunrise - a poet's creation!

6. Songs Upon the Aurora

Sing to me sweetly,
to whither away the melancholy,
The emptiness?
The loneliness?
Melt them away!

Clear my mind as I listen to you,
bring upon me those blessed tunes,
sway within my eyes
upon the starry skies,
draw me and my spirit to join with you,
so my notes can flow anew.

7. Drawing Lines

To calm my storms,
to ease my soul,
every thought takes its form,
every movement makes it whole -
what I see,
what I feel,
every breath,
from start to end -
just drawing lines,
in order to feel fine.

8. Paradise Dilo

You heard the songs they sing at night,
while you roam, you're treading light.
All the echoes, the chorus bring,
from the darkness forth a sweeter thing,

Lo! these Sirens do lure my wander heart,
to pause in tune and bear my part,
for the night so lonesome with nought to share,
Dilo sing, I will join you there.

9. Gadget

The shimmer of your soul
That hides the blood stain
Carries your voice
Through the storm and the rain;

Saw the drops that passed your eyes
As you looked up at the skies...

Seems that warmer smile
That lasted that little while -
Carried all your laughter
That hid all your pain,

10. Ocean of Pain

(A Dolphin's Song)

Yet it ends like this:
Some of life's secrets I miss.
Take me away from this –
This sad, polluted abyss!
Give me freedom of the mind,
Shall I seek, will I find?
The knowledge hidden within me is deep,
would I find, should I keep?
Take me back to blue waters,
here where my ships once had faltered.
Yes! Take me away to there,
this life mystery we all share.
Deep within this dark abyss,
I had wandered, this I'll miss.
Yet, it all ends like this!
Here, in this sad, polluted abyss...

11. Let me Touch the Sky

A broken whisper in the pen,
the spoken words of here and then,
the birds that fly they sing to me,
I am not like they are free,
the gentle winds they sing their song,
my heart still glows but not as strong,
my spirit torn and my the ink lay bare,
leaves me empty with less comfort there

Hear my song, oh shadows pry,
hear my call, this poet cries,
bring to me the warmth of Bleed,
bring to me some words to sing!

Silence still I want to be,
cast not forth my fate to me,
bear me down, bear me down to see,
Touch the Sky, I ask of thee!!

The silence hangs, my thoughts surmise,
the words had spoke and caught my eyes,
my tongue I've held I should have bit,
know not why I said I did..

Hear my song, oh shadows pry,
hear my call, this poet cries,
bring to me the warmth of Bleed,
bring to me some words to sing!

Silence still I want to be,
cast not forth my fate to me,
bear me down, bear me down to see,
Touch the Sky, I ask of thee!!

Here I stand, the lights do glow,
the warmth of me I hold to Flow,
the love I see they all must know,
before it ends and I must go.

Hear my song, oh shadows pry,
hear my call, this poet cries,
bring to me the warmth of Bleed,
bring to me some words to sing!

Silence still I want to be,
cast not forth my fate to me,
bear me down, bear me down to see,
Touch the Sky, I ask of thee!!

12. The Finger's Dance

Sometimes I wish I could draw
all that I dream and saw,
draw much more than words,
create tapestries of wonderful worlds;

Weave my hands and let the colors flow,
of places where I long to go,
of images that I always see
when a song catches and pulls at me,

of creatures both majestic or vile,
let my soul carry my ambitious style
and guide me to this paper pile;

where lies ideas and concepts, incompleted art,
lyrics and sonnets and poems in part,
memories and miseries and plans to make do
of all my ambitions and goals that stuck like glue

if only I could draw and create
while I procrastinate
in my times as I sit and lay with all my ideas
to release all my tensions and draw all my peers

where we dance in the meadows as our counterhearts
sing
and dragons abundant dance in my dream
where mountains of gold and meadows of green
flow through my fingers with all that I see
and in my Voice it would quiver like a harp's strongest
tune
on the wind it would carry till the third triplet moon,
where dolphins would play
in the Lullabye Bay
and serpents would swim
with their masses of kin,

if my hands could so pure draw
all that I saw
while I wrote all these words,
oh how I ache so it hurts
that one day my fingers could do more than just dance
as I realise it all when I take that chance.

13. Under Aurora Skies

Weep your Lines, little one,
why burden with this world?
For even the dark gives way to sun
no need for this guilt and hurt.

Sing your song to the moon this hour,
may the aurora dance and sway!
Be not alone, let your friends empower,
comfort in their presence today.

14. When the wind does fall

Close your eyes,
Close your eyes,
go to sleep, my dear,
when you need me I am by your side

Nestle close,
nestle close
I will never go,
even if the wind does ever fall

when dilos sing by Lune's deep tonight,
I will sing - I will sing with them as well;
for my song, for our song, it's a song for you,
even if the wind does ever fall

You're my precious one

don't you fear,
don't you fear,
I'll be always there

even as the wind does fade away,

don't you cry,
don't you cry,
I'll be always close,
I'll for ever be right your side

As dilos sing by Lune's deep tonight,
I will sing - I will sing with them as well;
for my song, for our song, it's a song for you,
even if the wind does ever fall

with you I will always be

Hear the dilos sing..
'neath aurora skies..
it's a song for you..
never fear

Little one,
precious one,
oh my precious dear..
may we sing together this last time

Little one,
precious one,
oh my precious dear..

may we share this one last song tonight,

As dilos sing by Lune's deep tonight,
we will sing - we will sing with them as well;
for our song, for our song, it's a song for you,
even if the wind does fall

with you I will always be

Hear the dilos sing..
'neath aurora skies..
it's a song for you..
always there

Hear my song, it's always there for you

15. Whittler

A page,
bare and blank,
my slate,
my tapestry, my plank.

Such little motions,
I draw upon her;
the little lines and shades,
the thoughts I confer,

The lands, the beings,
the worlds and its things,
the mountains and forests
'neath ancient dragon wings,

To the page I lay the colors
my pencil would fabricate,
from within it my soul uncovers,
all the magic it would create.

16. The Oro's Lullaby

Nestle close, my little darlings,
nestle close my dears,
nestle close to your mamma
let me chase those fears,

my little darlings don't you worry
they won't come near.
for I'll keep you close now
don't you shed those tears

My sweet lil younglings, don't you weep,
may the dilos sing to bring you sleep,
lay sweet darlings,
I'll keep you warm,
through this night,
so your dreams are brighter
than the aurora light

17. Pencil's Edge

On a Pencil's edge,
What to sketch.
I've got this itch,
Can you show me, Teach?

I want to guide my thoughts
From words to draughts,
Give more life to my rhyme,
to bring wonder in time.

I want to feel, more than words;
bound in sight the merry and hurts,
spread the worlds my spirit wander
From their seas to the individual wonder,

On a Pencil's edge,
What to sketch,
From a chior of singing dilo,
Or the cuddle of affectionate oro,

the elegance of the allo,
Or the strong embrace of the giga we know,
The cackle of the austro fair,
Or the gathering of herds somewhere

Or the plains of the scrapes that fill my world;
Where dragons roam with wings unfurled,
Where twin rise to three moon skies,
The heirkin reign, and progress surprise,

The fairest maidens to the most lowly being,
from the royal to the humble, to bring,
on a pencil's edge..
What to sketch,
What to etch..

18. The Dilo's Audience

Mayhap I stay my distance,
Mayhap I stay my song,
Mayhap I haven't resistance
When their melody speaks so strong

There is no doubt or shadow
When their calls sound out at night,
Be it upon Murky's shallows
or 'neath Radio's Light.

So few calls ring a melody
to make me pause to listen glee,
So few bring my heart a-fluttering
to embrace the night, and set me free

Mayhap these calls are chilling:
for many a warning sound;
For my soul it's so fulfilling
to listen: tranquil, delighted, bound;

Mayhap I'd make appearance,
Yes, I will stay around,
I'm with no hesitance;
I will join your sound

19. Grace me with Song

Grace me with your song tonight,
dilo
I seek the freedom of your lyrics,
you know,
the wind..
the moon,
the rivers and seas,
whenever you break the silence,
there descends a peace.

I seek your calm melodies,
seek your charm,
its soothing caress
as I submit to your chorus,
that consumes my troubles,
makes me calm.

Dilo..
Would you break the silence of the night,
with me as your audience in the aurora light?
My voice, though broken,
a little worn,
would join your calls till the daylight morn.
Help me let go,
dilo,
with the only way that you know.

20. A Journey to the Past

A window to the ancient,
through the songs I've revisit,
to the melodies on the wind
and the scars that still persist,
from the thoughts, and musings
to the pain and the bruisings.

For all the memories in over a thousand,
and the many a thousand that predates those;
for every line in every word I've ever penned down-
a tapestry of verses to visually resend.

In every moment as I walked through these forests
so many views of myself, even the smallest,
a paw print to the heart and a song to the mind,
how I sought it all, and how I'd find

that the journey from the first word upon the canvas of
white,
despite the regrets of surrendering my Artist's Sight,
the Touch of the verse and the songs of the soul -
would lead me anew into a future of gold

21. Everything

My universe,
I gaze upon the heavens,
and I see you -
you grace the sky,
you grace the stars,
you are so like them,
grand, so unfathomably grand,
and so far from my reach, my friend -
you are the one I wish to settle by,
the one desire to strengthen my light.
Beyond my stead, beyond my reach -
you're the winds above that would one day guide my
flight;
I do so yearn to be with you, on this night

22. Serenades of the Tides

rock it steady,
every step,
now more than ever,
ebb those regrets,
grains of time hold no value,
a serenade will calm your blues,
dawn is just a whisper away,
every moment is here to stay,
settle your soul, within my embrace

oh, sweetheart of my song,
follow into my melodies,
travel to the horizon wide,
heaven's golden tapestries
erase the darkness of the night -

travel to the horizon wide,
into my melodies sweetest one,
draw upon the growing light -
every breath, every step, towards the sun

23. Beyond the spread of your wings

beyond the breath,
the moment,
the beat;
the sky,
the wind,
to meet,
soar ye high,
may thy soul dance in the skies,
may thy song bless the winds;
thou tune fill the silent forests,
thy wings comfort those bereft,
may thy soar ever higher, ever more,
brighter than the heavens stars,
may thee find peace, eternal,
and in thou rest, a nest, to comfort those thee had
touched - ever more

24. Well

Dear friend
It's time we art,
You and I,
For a brand new start
You're the insight that sustains,
The inspiration that remains,
The will that I can rely upon,
The voice of seasons when there stirs a song
I will be the guide to flow your paths,
the eyes that see where you can't pass,
The soul that would bear your notes on high,
and the ties that mould us, you and I

25. Aurora's Song

Into the solar winds,
we set our course -
where the old world ends,
the new world begins,
we follow the tides
through the black and white,
cradled by her wings
we seek the light;

The songs of silence
she sent so long,
to seek the guidance
to hold her strong
determined defiance
against all gone wrong,
for the last of the titans
brings Aurora's song

So find the stars
to bring you day,
to guide you far
through the Milkyway,
for your wings to spread
and your voice be heard,
beyond the waves of dread
and seas of hurt -

The songs of silence
she sent so long,
to seek the guidance
to hold her strong
determined defiance
against all gone wrong;
for the last of the titans
brings Aurora's song

26. Exploration of the Mind

Upon a moment bright
a line to hold the sight
for a moment there to shine
to grasp,
to seize,
to wind;

Upon that moment bright
the sparks would so ignite -
from words and lines
to rhythms,
for dreams,
to shine.